Amahl and the Night Visitors

Amahl
and the Night Visitors

By GIAN CARLO MENOTTI   Illustrated by MICHÈLE LEMIEUX

WILLIAM MORROW AND COMPANY, INC.

NEW YORK

Text © 1986 by William Morrow and Company, Inc.
Adapted from *Amahl and the Night Visitors* by Gian Carlo Menotti © 1951, 1952, 1980 by G. Schirmer, Inc.
Illustrations © 1986 Michèle Lemieux.

1 2 3 4 5 6 7 8 9 10

Library of Congress Cataloging in Publication Data
Menotti, Gian Carlo, 1911-   Amahl and the night visitors.
Summary: Relates how a crippled young shepherd comes to accompany the three Kings on their way to pay
homage to the newborn Jesus. 1. Children's stories, American. [1. Jesus Christ—Nativity—Fiction. 2.
Christmas—Fiction] I. Lemieux, Michèle, ill. II. Title.
PZ7.M53Am   1986   [Fic]   84-27196
ISBN 0-688-05426-9 I ISBN 0-688-05427-7 (lib. bdg.)

Music from a shepherd's pipe filled the cold winter air. Wrapped in a heavy cloak, a boy sat in the evening shadow, piping steadily. As he played, stars appeared in the darkening sky. The boy could see that one star burned more brightly than the others, and he could not take his eyes from it. He did not hear his mother call him from the small house nearby.

A moment later, she called again. "Amahl! Time to go to bed!"

Amahl put down his shepherd's pipe. "Coming," he answered, but he did not move. Instead, he raised his pipe and began to play again.

A woman leaned out of one of the windows of the cottage. "How long must I shout before you obey?"

Amahl stopped piping. "I'm sorry, Mother."

"Hurry in. It's time to go to bed." His mother sounded impatient.

"Mother, let me stay a little longer," Amahl said.

"The wind is cold," his mother objected.

"But my cloak is warm," Amahl answered.

"The night is dark," said his mother.

"But the sky is light," Amahl argued.

"The time is late," Amahl's mother insisted.

"But the moon hasn't risen yet. Let me stay a little longer." Amahl was almost begging.

His mother clapped her hands together sharply. "There won't be a moon tonight. But there will be a weeping child very soon if he doesn't hurry up and obey his mother." She shut the window with a bang.

"Oh, very well." Amahl picked up the crutch lying beside him on the ground. Leaning on it heavily, he limped into the house. He hung his cloak and hat on pegs and placed his pipe carefully on the mantle. Amahl returned to the open doorway to watch the blazing star once more.

"What was keeping you outside?" his mother asked from near the fireplace, where she was trying to coax a flame from some twigs.

Amahl turned toward his mother. "Oh, Mother, you should go out and see! There's never been such a sky!" Amahl limped across the room, talking excitedly. "Hanging over our roof there is a star as large as a window. The star has a tail, and it moves across the sky like a chariot on fire."

Amahl's mother sighed. "Oh, Amahl," she said wearily, "when will you stop telling lies? All day long you wander about in a dream." She glanced about the bare room. "Here we are with nothing to eat, not a stick of wood on the fire, not a drop of oil in the jug, and all you do is to worry your mother with fairy tales." She looked very serious as she said, "Oh, Amahl, have you forgotten your promise never, never to lie to your mother again?"

"Mother, I'm not lying," said Amahl. "Please believe me." He took hold of her skirt. "Come outside and let me show you. See for yourself."

Amahl's mother freed her skirt from his grasp. "Stop bothering me! Why should I believe you?" Her voice was rough. "You come at me with a new one every day! First it was a leopard with a woman's head. Then it was a tree branch that shrieked and bled. Then it was a fish as big as a boat, with whiskers like a cat and wings like a bat and horns like a goat. And now it is a star as large as a window—or was it a carriage? And if that wasn't enough, the star has a tail, and the tail is made of fire!"

"But there is a star," Amahl persisted, "and it has a tail this long." He held out his arms as wide as he could. When he saw his mother frowning, he brought his arms closer together. "Well, only this long. But it's there!"

"*Amahl.*" His mother's voice was reproving.

"Cross my heart and hope to die," Amahl said.

Putting her arms around her son, Amahl's mother said, "Poor Amahl, hunger has gone to your head."

She went on, more to herself than to Amahl. "Dear God, what is a poor widow to do when her cupboards and pockets are empty and everything is sold?" She sank onto a small stool. "Unless we go begging how shall we live through tomorrow?" Amahl's mother wept. "My little son, a beggar!" she said.

"Don't cry, Mother dear, don't worry for me." Amahl knelt by her side. "If we must go begging, a good beggar I'll be. I'll play sweet tunes to set people dancing. We'll walk and walk from village to town, you dressed as a gypsy and I as a clown." Amahl glanced at his shepherd's pipe in its place on the mantel. "I'll play my pipe, you'll sing and you'll shout. The windows will open and people will lean out. The king will ride by and hear your loud voice and throw us some gold to stop all the noise." Amahl and his mother tried to smile. They each knew he was trying to cheer them with the thought of the king throwing gold to quiet them. Amahl continued with longing in his voice, for there had been no supper, "At noon we shall eat roast goose and sweet almonds, at night we shall sleep with the sheep and the stars."

Amahl's mother took him in her arms. "My dreamer, good night!"

Amahl kissed his mother and lay down on his straw mat, his crutch nearby. Covering Amahl with his cloak,

his mother lay down on the bench near the fireplace and was soon asleep.

Awake in the dark room, Amahl heard singing in the distance.

From far away we come and farther we must go.
How far, how far, my crystal star?

Amahl raised himself onto one elbow. The singing was closer.

The shepherd dreams inside the fold.
Cold are the sands by the silent sea.
Frozen the incense in our frozen hands,
Heavy the gold.

Amahl threw back his cloak, found his crutch, and hobbled to the window. At first he saw nothing, although the singing continued.

From far away we come and farther we must go.
How far, how far, my crystal star?

At the window, Amahl watched as a magnificent caravan approached his house. Three stately camels carrying three richly dressed men moved past Amahl at his window and then came to a stop.

There was a knock at the door.

Amahl's mother did not stir from the bench. "Amahl," she said, "go and see who's knocking at the door."

"Yes, Mother." Amahl hobbled to the door and opened it a crack. One of the richly dressed men from the caravan was standing before him. Up close, Amahl could see the man was wearing a crown. Amahl stared for a moment. Then he quickly closed the door and hurried to his mother.

"Mother, Mother, Mother," Amahl called as he limped across the room, "come with me. I want to be sure you see what I see."

Sitting up, Amahl's mother asked, "What is the matter with you? What is all the fuss about? Who is it?"

"Mother," Amahl said hesitantly, "outside the door there is . . . there is a king with a crown."

Amahl's mother seemed to be talking to the ceiling. "What shall I do with this boy? What shall I do?" She looked at Amahl. "If you don't learn to tell the truth, I'll have to spank you."

There was a second knock at the door. "Go back and see who it is and ask them what they want," Amahl's mother said, and she lay down once more.

Amahl opened the door a crack and peered through it.

Again he made his way back to his mother, saying, "Mother, Mother, Mother, come with me. I want to be sure you see what I see."

"What is the matter with you now?" asked his mother. "What is all the fuss about?"

"Mother," Amahl said, "I didn't tell the truth before."

His mother patted his arm. "That's a good boy."

"There is not a king outside," said Amahl.

"I should say not," said Amahl's mother.

"There are two kings!" Amahl held his breath, waiting for his mother's reaction.

"What shall I do with this boy, what shall I do?" Amahl's mother wailed. Then she ordered him, "Hurry back and see who it is, and don't you dare make up tales!"

For the third time, Amahl hobbled to the door, looked out, and returned to his mother saying, "Mother, Mother, Mother, come with me." He paused. "If I tell you the truth, I know you won't believe me."

"Try it for a change," said his mother.

"But you won't believe me," Amahl told her.

"I'll believe you if you tell the truth," said his mother.

Amahl took a deep breath. "Sure enough," he said, "there aren't two kings outside."

"That is not surprising," Amahl's mother said.

"There are three kings," Amahl announced, "and one of them is black!"

"Oh! What shall I do with this boy!" Amahl's mother was very angry. "If you were stronger, I'd whip you."

"I knew it," Amahl muttered under his breath.

Amahl's mother rose from the bench.

"I'm going to the door myself, and then, young man, you'll have to reckon with me!"

As the door swung open, Amahl's mother gasped and then bowed low, for standing in the doorway were three

men dressed in royal splendor. Each king carried a
treasure: one a softly burnished chalice of myrrh, one a
gleaming urn of incense, and one an elaborate coffer
of gold.

"Good evening." The Three Kings spoke together.

"What did I tell you?" Amahl whispered to his mother.

"*Shh,*" his mother hissed in Amahl's direction, and to the kings she said, "Noble sires."

"May we rest awhile in your house and warm ourselves by your fireplace?" asked the black king.

"I am a poor widow. All I can offer you are a cold fireplace and a bed of straw. But to these you are welcome," Amahl's mother replied.

One of the kings appeared to be deaf. Cupping a hand over his ear, he asked the other two, "What did she say?"

"That we are welcome," answered the black king.

"Oh, thank you, thank you, thank you," said the deaf king excitedly, and he would have continued, but the other kings tapped him on his shoulders, and he finally became quieted down. Then, speaking together, the three kings said, "Oh, thank you."

Bowing again, Amahl's mother said, "Come in, come in!"

A page, carrying a lantern, entered first. He was bent almost double under the baggage he carried on his back, which included an Oriental rug, a parrot in a cage, and a beautiful jeweled box.

Carefully lowering the baggage to the floor, the page hurried to the doorway, where the kings still stood. Picking up the train of the deaf king, the page announced

loudly, "King Kaspar," and the page and the deaf king marched to the fireplace. The page rushed back to the doorway to carry the train of the black king. "King Balthazar," the page said respectfully, and the black king joined Kaspar. The page darted to the door to escort the third king into the room. "King Melchior," he said. The page spread the beautiful Oriental rug and placed on it the riches each king carried.

"It is nice here," said Melchior, looking around the room.

Amahl's mother reached for her shawl. "I shall go and gather wood for the fire. I've nothing in the house."

"We can only stay a little while," said Melchior. "We must not lose sight of our star."

"Your star?" asked Amahl's mother.

"What did I tell you?" Amahl whispered to her.

"*Shh!*" his mother whispered in return. Then, speaking aloud, she said, "I'll be right back . . . and Amahl, don't be a nuisance."

"No, Mother." As soon as the door closed behind her, Amahl approached Balthazar.

"Are you a real king?" he asked, leaning on his crutch.

"Yes," said Balthazar.

"Have you regal blood?" asked Amahl.

"Yes," Balthazar answered.

"Can I see it?" Amahl asked.

"It is just like yours," said Balthazar.

"What's the use of having it then?" asked Amahl.

"No use," was Balthazar's answer.

"Where is your home?" asked Amahl.

"I live in a black marble palace, full of black panthers and white doves," said Balthazar. "And you, little boy, what do you do?"

"I was a shepherd," Amahl said sadly to Balthazar. "I had a flock of sheep, but my mother sold them. Now there are no sheep left. I had a black goat who gave me warm, sweet milk. But she died of old age, and now there is no goat left."

Turning to Kaspar who was feeding his parrot, Amahl asked, "Are you a real king, too?"

"Eh?" said Kaspar.

Puzzled by Kaspar's response, Amahl looked questioningly at Balthazar, who signaled that Kaspar had trouble hearing.

Amahl repeated his question, shouting, "Are you a real king, too?"

"Oh, truly, truly yes. I am a real king." Kaspar seemed very sure of himself. But then he turned to Balthazar. "Am I not?"

"Yes, Kaspar," said Balthazar.

"What is that?" asked Amahl, pointing to the parrot.

"Eh?" said Kaspar.

Shouting, Amahl repeated his question.

"A parrot," said Kaspar.

"Does it talk?" asked Amahl.

"Eh?" said Kaspar.

"Does it talk?" shouted Amahl.

"How do I know?" asked Kaspar, pointing to his ears.

"Does it bite?" asked Amahl.

"Eh?"

"Does it bite?" shouted Amahl.

"Yes," said Kaspar, and he held up a bandaged finger.

"And what is this?" asked Amahl, pointing to the beautiful jeweled box.

Holding up the box and speaking with excitement, Kaspar said to Amahl, "This is my box, this is my box, I never travel without my box." He opened the top drawer. "In the first drawer I keep my magic stones." Kaspar held each stone in turn before Amahl's dazzled eyes and said, "One carnelian against all evil and envy, one moonstone to make you sleep, one red coral to heal your wounds, one lapis lazuli against winter fever, one small jasper to help you find water, one small topaz to soothe your eyes, and one red ruby to protect you from lightning."

Kaspar opened the next drawer. "In the second drawer I keep all my beads." He brought out handfuls of beads while Amahl stared. "Oh, how I love to play with beads, all kinds of beads."

Kaspar could hardly bring himself to put the beads away, but finally he closed the bead drawer and opened the next, saying slowly, "In the third drawer . . . " He paused, and Amahl could hardly hear Kaspar as he said, "Oh, little boy, in the third drawer I keep . . . " Kaspar took a deep breath and smiled broadly at Amahl. "Licorice!" he said happily, "black sweet licorice. Have some." He thrust the drawer at Amahl, who grabbed a piece and was swallowing the last of it when his mother returned.

"Amahl, I told you not to be a nuisance," she scolded.

"But it isn't my fault," Amahl protested. Then hobbling toward her, he whispered, "They kept asking me questions."

"I want you to go out and call the shepherds," said his mother. "Tell them about our visitors and ask them to bring whatever they have in their houses, as we have nothing to offer them. Hurry!"

"Yes, Mother." Amahl wrapped his cloak about him and put on his hat. Leaning on his crutch, he limped out as quickly as he could.

His mother moved toward the gleaming coffer of gold and the rich chalices of myrrh and incense spread out before the kings. "Oh, these beautiful things," she exclaimed, "and all that gold!"

"These are gifts to the Child," Melchior told her.

"The child?" asked Amahl's mother. "Which child?"

"We don't know," said Melchior. "But the Star will guide us to Him."

"Perhaps I know him," said Amahl's mother. "What does he look like?"

"Have you seen a child the color of wheat, the color of dawn?" asked Melchior. "His eyes are mild, and his hands are those of a king. We are bringing incense, myrrh, and gold to Him, and the Eastern Star is our guide."

Amahl's mother answered softly, "Yes, I know a child the color of wheat, the color of dawn. His eyes are mild, and his hands are those of a king. But no one will bring him incense or gold, though he may be sick and poor and hungry and cold." She paused for a moment. "He's my child, my son, my darling, my own."

Melchior stretched out a hand. "The Child we seek holds the seas and the winds on His palm," he said.

"The child we seek has the moon and the stars at His feet," said Kaspar.

And Balthazar added, "Before Him the eagle is gentle, the lion is meek."

Going to the door and looking out for Amahl, his mother said softly, "The child I know holds my hand on his palm, the child I know has my life at his feet. He's my child, my son, my darling, my own, and his name is Amahl."

The room became quiet—so quiet that Kaspar dozed off. Suddenly, a sharp call was heard.

"The shepherds are coming," Amahl's mother told the Kings.

Melchior nudged the sleeping Kaspar. "Wake up!"

From the doorway Amahl's mother saw lanterns brightening the dark night. Led by Amahl, shepherds and their families gathered to honor the kings and bring them gifts. As the shepherds approached Amahl's house, they greeted each other loudly.

"Emily, Michael, Bartholomew, how are your children and how are your sheep?"

"Dorothy, Peter, Evangeline, come along. We are going with Amahl, bringing gifts to the kings."

"Benjamin, Lucas, Elizabeth, how are your children and how are your sheep?"

"Carolyn, Matthew, Veronica, give me your hand, come along. The night is so cold! The wind is so icy! Your cloak is so warm!"

"Katherine, Christopher, Babila, how are your children and how are your sheep?"

"Josephine, Angela, Jeremy, come along."

The shepherds crowded into the doorway of Amahl's house.

"Oh! Look! Look!" they said to each other. They were so overcome by the splendor of the kings, they felt afraid to enter.

Amahl squeezed his way through them and took his place next to his mother, who encouraged the shepherds, saying, "Come in, come in! What are you scared of? Don't be bashful! Show what you brought them."

"Go on, go on, go on," the shepherds said to one another. "No! You go on."

From the center of the group one man approached the kings. He bowed and set a tray before them. "Olives and quinces, apples and raisins, nutmeg and myrtle, persimmons and chestnuts, this is all we shepherds can offer you," he said, and then took his place among the shepherds again.

"Thank you, thank you, thank you kindly," said the Three Kings in unison.

A second shepherd approached the kings and, after bowing, set another tray before them. "Citrons and lemons, musk and pomegranates, goat cheese and walnuts, figs and cucumbers, this is all we shepherds can offer you," the man said to the kings.

"Thank you, thank you, thank you kindly," the kings said, again speaking as one.

A third shepherd approached the kings and presented his gifts. "Hazelnuts and camomile, mignonette and laurel, honeycombs and cinnamon, thyme, mint, and garlic, this is all we shepherds can offer you," he said, and again the Three Kings, speaking together, said, "Thank you, thank you, thank you kindly, too."

41

"Take them, eat them, you are welcome," said a shepherd to the kings, while another shepherd repeated to the page, "Take them, eat them, you are welcome, too."

"Now won't you dance for the kings?" Amahl's mother asked some of the shepherds. One young girl was embarrassed and tried to flee. But the young men nudged and pulled her back, and she returned to the group. Reaching for his shepherd's pipe, Amahl joined an elderly man at the fireplace, where the two began to play. Shyly at first, a few shepherds danced before the kings. As they danced, the shepherds grew confident and soon others joined in joyously.

Amahl and the old man piped every dance tune they knew, matching their music to the whirling dancers.

At the end, it was Balthazar who rose from his place and said, "Thank you, good friends, for your dance and your gifts. But now we must bid you good night. We have little time for sleep and a long journey tomorrow."

Bowing as they passed before the kings, the shepherds filed out of Amahl's house, singing as they went.

Good night, my good kings, good night and farewell,
The pale stars foretell that dawn is in sight.
Good night, my good kings, good night and farewell.
The night wind foretells the day will be bright.

The shepherds' voices became faint in the night air.

In the house, the kings settled themselves for sleep near the fireplace. While Amahl's mother was preparing a pallet for herself on the floor, Amahl saw a chance to speak with Kaspar without her noticing. Limping across the room, he said to the king, "Excuse me, sir, among your magic stones is there . . . " Amahl paused, "is there one that could cure a crippled boy?"

"Eh?" Once again, Kaspar did not hear him. Amahl turned away sadly. "Never mind . . . good night."

The shepherds' song drifted into the darkened, quiet room.

Good night, good night,
The dawn is in sight.
Good night, farewell, good night.

Amahl and his mother on their pallets, the Three Kings
huddled together, and the page curled up on the rug near
the gold, listened as the shepherds' last notes lingered
in the stillness. Soon nearly everyone was asleep.

Only Amahl's mother was awake, sitting stiffly on her pallet, staring at the treasure guarded by the Page.

"All that gold!" she thought. "I wonder if rich people know what to do with their gold? Do the rich know how a child could be fed? Do they know that a house can be kept warm all day with burning logs? Do they know how to roast sweet corn on the fire, how to milk a clover-fed goat, how to spice hot wine on cold winter nights?"

Amahl's mother raised herself to her knees and moved closer to the gold. "Oh, what I could do for my child with that gold! Why," she asked herself, "should it all go to a child they don't even know?" She crept even closer to the riches.

In a trembling voice Amahl's mother said aloud, "They are asleep. Do I dare? If I take some, they'll never miss it."

She stretched herself toward the gold, murmuring, "For my child . . . for my child . . . for my child . . . "

In an instant the page was awake. He grabbed Amahl's mother, shouting to the kings, "Thief, thief!" Her hands full of gold and jewels, Amahl's mother tried to free herself from the page, and the two of them dragged each other into the center of the room, fighting all the while.

"What is it?" asked the kings, rising from the bench in confusion.

"I've seen her steal some of the gold," the page panted as he struggled with Amahl's mother. "She's a thief! She's stolen the gold!"

"Shame! Shame!" the kings cried.

"Give it back, or I'll tear it out of you," snarled the page.

When Amahl awakened and saw his mother and the page battling with each other, he grabbed his crutch and threw himself on the man, beating him and pulling his hair.

"Don't you dare hurt my mother! I'll smash in your face! I'll knock out your teeth! Don't you dare hurt my mother," Amahl shouted.

Frantically, Amahl hobbled to Kaspar and tugged on his robe. "Oh, don't let him hurt my mother! My mother is good. She cannot do anything wrong. I'm the one who lies. I'm the one who steals."

As fast as he could, Amahl limped back to the page, shouting, "Don't you dare hurt my mother! I'll break all your bones! I'll bash in your head!"

Kaspar signaled to the page to leave Amahl's mother alone. She knelt and held out her arms to Amahl. Sobbing, he went into her arms, letting his crutch fall to the floor.

Melchior stood over the two of them. "Oh, woman," he said, "you may keep the gold. The Child we seek doesn't need our gold. He will build his kingdom on love alone. His hand will not hold a scepter, his head will not wear a crown. His might will not be built by your toil." Melchior turned to Kaspar and Balthazar. "Let us leave, my friends."

Freeing herself from Amahl, his mother rushed toward the kings and knelt before them, spilling the gold she had taken onto the floor. "Oh, no, wait—take your gold! I've waited all my life for such a king. And if I weren't so poor, I would send a gift of my own to such a child."

"Mother," said Amahl, "let me send Him my crutch. Who knows, he may need one, and this I made myself." Amahl offered his crutch to the kings.

Horrified, his mother said, "But you can't! You can't!" as Amahl, with his crutch still raised, took a step forward. A hush fell over the room. Holding his crutch in his outstretched hands, Amahl took another step. Breaking the silence Amahl whispered, "I walk, Mother . . . Mother, I walk!"

"He walks . . . " said the Three Kings, together.

"He walks . . . " said Amahl's mother, rising to her feet, never taking her eyes from Amahl as he advanced steadily toward the kings, holding his crutch before him. As he placed it in Kaspar's hands, the Three Kings spoke. "It is a sign from the Holy Child. We must give praise to the newborn King."

Amahl walked to the center of the room. At first his steps were slow, but soon he moved faster. "Look, Mother, I can dance, I can jump, I can run!" he called.

"Truly, he can dance, he can jump, he can run," the Three Kings echoed.

His mother ran after Amahl, afraid he might fall and hurt himself. When he stumbled, his mother quickly caught him, saying, "Please, my darling, be careful now. You must not hurt yourself."

"Oh, good woman, you must not be afraid," the kings told her, "for he is loved by the Son of God."

Kaspar stepped forward. "Oh, blessed child, may we touch you?" he asked. Amahl nodded yes. The Three Kings passed before Amahl and laid their hands on his head. Then each King picked up his gift to the Christ Child and prepared to leave, for it was time to continue their journey.

The page hung back and then approached Amahl, bowing low. "Oh, blessed child, may I touch you?" he asked. Gazing at the man who had so recently mistreated his mother, Amahl said, "Well, I don't know if I'm going to let *you* touch me."

"Amahl!" said his mother.

"Oh, all right," Amahl told the page. "But just once." The page came forward and touched Amahl's hand very quickly.

Turning to his mother, Amahl said, "Look, Mother, I can fight, I can work, I can play. Oh, Mother, let me go with the kings. I want to take my crutch to the Child myself."

"Yes, good woman, let him come with us," the kings said. "We'll take good care of him, and we'll bring him home on a camel's back."

Putting her arms around Amahl, his mother asked, "Do you really want to go?"

"Yes, Mother," said Amahl.

"Are you sure, sure, sure?" asked his mother.

"I'm sure," said Amahl.

"Yes," she said, smiling at him, "I think you should go and bring thanks to the Child yourself."

Surprised, Amahl asked, "Are you sure, sure, sure?"

"Go on, get ready," his mother said, and Amahl hurried away to collect what he needed for his journey.

The Three Kings had been listening. "What did she say?" Kaspar asked the other two.

"She said he can come," said Balthazar.

"Oh, lovely, lovely, lov—" Kaspar began excitedly, but he stopped when Balthazar laid a hand on his shoulder and said sternly "Kaspar!"

As he put on his warm cloak, Amahl's mother reminded him, "Don't forget to wear your hat."

"I shall always wear my hat," Amahl assured her.

"Wash your ears," she said.

"Yes, I promise."

"Don't tell lies."

"No, I promise."

Softly, Amahl and his mother said to each other, "I shall miss you very much."

"Are you ready?" Melchior asked Amahl.

"Yes, I'm ready," Amahl answered.

"Let's go then." Melchior and Amahl took their places behind Kaspar and Balthazar and the page, who once more was bent double under the weight of the baggage on his back.

The caravan waited outside the house. On their camels, the kings looked more imposing than ever. Amahl hurried back to his mother to say good-bye one more time. Then the page helped him onto Kaspar's camel. With jingling bridles, the camels moved forward. Amahl waved to his mother. Standing in the doorway of their house and smiling, she waved back.

The caravan turned a corner, and Amahl could no longer see his mother or his house. Leaning against Kaspar, he brought out his shepherd's pipe and began to play. He piped all the songs he knew. He piped first for the Christ Child, then for the kings, next for his mother, for the shepherds, for the parrot—even for the page. And as he piped, the caravan moved onward.